Fun Bug Facts for Kids

Jacquelyn Elnor Johnson

www.CrimsonHillBooks.com

© 2024 Crimson Hill Books/Crimson Hill Products Inc.

All rights reserved worldwide. No part of this book, including words and illustrations, maybe be copied, lent for publication, excerpted, licensed, quoted nor used for artificial intelligence (AI) training. No robots nor any other form of AI were involved in any aspect of creating this work.

First edition, March 2024.

Cataloguing in Publication Data

Johnson, Jacquelyn Elnor

Fun Bug Facts for Kids

Description: Crimson Hill Books trade hardcover edition | Nova Scotia, Canada

ISBN:	978-1-990887-07-9 (Hardcover - Ingram)
BISAC:	JNF003000 Juvenile Fiction: Animals – General JNF003120 Juvenile Fiction: Animals – Insects, Spiders, Etc. JNF003170 Juvenile Nonfiction: Animals - Pets
THEMA:	WNGX - Insects & spiders as pets WNCN - Wildlife: butterflies, other insects and spiders: general interest YNNL - Children's - Teenage general interest: Insects, spiders, minibeasts

Record available at https://www.bac-lac.gc.ca/eng/Pages/home.aspx

Book design: Jesse Johnson

Crimson Hill Books
(a division of)
Crimson Hill Products Inc.
Lawrencetown, Nova Scotia
Canada

Fun Bug Facts for Kids

Some can fly.

Some have jobs in their bug cities.

Some astonish us with their beauty.

BUGS are bizarre!

Insects, or BUGS to use their nickname, are small. They're everywhere. And they're really odd. Some people think they're the strangest creatures on earth.

All insects belong to the much larger family of animals called Arthropods. Other members in this family, all distant cousins of the insect clan, are spiders, lobsters and millipedes.

Bugs live nearly everywhere on earth. You can find them in forests and fields, in trees and on plants. Some live with us, in our buildings and houses. And some can live underwater.

Others like these beetles are never going to win any bug beauty contests.

On earth, it's the bugs that rule!

There are more species of bugs, and more bugs in total than any other animal alive today.

Some bugs are plant-eaters, while others are meat-eaters.

Bugs live almost everywhere on earth.

Most insects prefer to live alone, but others like Ants, Bees and Termites live in huge colonies.

Insects do many jobs that are useful to people. They create honey, pollinate plants including food crops, make dead animals and plants decompose and help keep the soil healthy. They're also food for many birds, reptiles, and mammals. But some bugs are also destructive to food crops, unwanted pests that bite or sting or even dangerous to animals and humans.

Insects were the first animals to evolve on land and the first to fly.

How many insects are alive right now?

We don't know exactly, but scientists estimate the total insect population of the world at 10 quintillion. Here's what that number looks like, written out:

10,000,000,000,000,000,000

You could add up all the people and animals on earth and there'd still be more bugs than every other living creature.

Bugs by Numbers

479 million	years insects have lived on earth (humans have been here for only about 300,000 years)
5.5 million	insect species we think there might be, but it could be as many as 30 million
1 million	insect species already discovered and named
91,000	known insect species in United States
7,000	new insect species are discovered every year
95	percentage of all animal species on earth that are insects

This is a Garden Tiger Moth. Not all insects are bugs. And some bugs aren't insects at all.

True bugs and false bugs

Centipedes, Millipedes, Woodlice, Pillbugs, Sowbugs, Spiders, Mites and Scorpions aren't bugs. They aren't even insects. They all belong to other animal families.

To be a true bug, you need to have a hard exoskeleton. This is a skeleton on the outside of your body. This body is in three parts. That's a head, a thorax that is the middle section and the largest section, the abdomen.

All insects have 6 legs and 2 antennae on their heads.

Adult insects are the only arthropods that have wings. Arthropods are the animal group that all have a hard exoskeleton.

Some bugs, like Earwigs, are good mothers, looking after their eggs and their babies.

Some bugs hibernate through the cold months of the year. Others migrate. Or they lay their eggs and die and the eggs become next year's adults.

Where did bugs come from?

Insects have been on earth for a very long time. They evolved long before humans and long before the dinosaurs. They first appeared on earth at the same time that plants that live on land did.

The first land insects probably evolved from crustaceans that lived in water. Then, about 380 million to 400 million years ago, one group of insects learned how to fly, the first animals able to do this.

With this new ability, insect numbers exploded because flight gave them a big advantage. Now, they could move further and faster. They could eat leaves at the tops of trees. They could also escape their predators faster.

The most dangerous Ant in the world is the Bulldog Ant. It lives in Australia. This Ant is large, aggressive, and it bites and stings with venom strong enough to kill a human.

Earth's climate has changed many times

In one period when there was more oxygen in the air than there is today, insects were able to become much larger. The largest insect that ever lived that we know of is *Meganeura monyi*, a giant Dragonfly. Its wings were 27 inches, or 68.5 centimetres, from wing tip to wing tip. It lived 325 million years ago.

Insects were among the first animals to eat plants. About a million years after the first insects appeared, plants began to have flowers. This was their strategy to attract the insects to visit, drawn by color, nectar and pollen. When the insects visited flowers, they were covered in pollen that they took with them to other flowers.

This is called pollination. It is still how most plants reproduce. Reproduce means making more new plants. It was a brilliant strategy by the plants to start having flowers and putting the bugs to work! Before then, all plants had to rely on the wind to spread their pollen. Now, with bug power, they could spread far further.

Over the many millions of years they have been here, insects have changed as the world's climate changed. Some types of insects, like the ancient giant Dragonflies, are now extinct.

When it gets colder than 55 degrees F. or 12.78 degrees C., Butterflies can't eat or fly.

Fun Bug Facts for Kids

Staying small is a bug superpower!

Why are all bugs so small?

The giant insects lived at a time when there was far more oxygen in the air. As the world's atmosphere and climate changed, bugs became smaller.

Being small gives bugs some huge advantages. Their smaller bodies need less energy to work, meaning bugs need less food to survive. They can hide from predators in smaller places. Some are so small they live their entire lives inside of other bugs!

Being small also means they can move faster and hide from their enemies more easily and in smaller spaces.

All insects have:

3 body parts – head, thorax and abdomen

6 legs with joints

2 antennae on their heads

1 exoskeleton

Our ancient human ancestors ate insects raw. Insects were plentiful, easy to catch and a healthy food because they are a good source of protein.

It's a bug's world!

Insects have a long history on earth, far longer than humans. What has helped them survive and thrive for so long, through many times of climate change when other animals, like the dinosaurs, were wiped out?

1. For some, it was learning to fly.
2. For some others, it is living in colonies, called hives.
3. Being small. They can live in places many other animals can't.
4. Their ability to quickly adapt to changes in the environment.
5. Their super abilities to reproduce (this means have lots of babies).
6. Having short lives. It means their kind can evolve more quickly.
7. Their close relationships with plants, especially flowering plants.

Evolve means changing, from one generation to the next, to have a better chance to survive. Sometimes this means gaining new skills. Or it could mean that body parts change. Species need to evolve quickly when the climate is changing, when a new predator appears or when their food sources change.

There is only one other animal besides humans that keeps another animal as a farm animal. That's ants, who keep aphids and milk them for honeydew.

Most insects have compound eyes, allowing them to see in every direction at the same time.

Strange eyes

The world that bugs see is very different than what humans see.

Almost all bugs can see the difference between light and dark. Many can see blue and green. Some can see other types of light and colors that humans can't see. We know bugs can see things in infrared and ultraviolet light, which has colors humans don't have names for. There might be other types of light we don't know about that animals can see.

Some insects, like Bees, can also see polarized light.

Some insects also have extra eyes, called simple eyes. These simple eyes can only detect light or dark. Their simple eyes might be on their faces, or for some species, the simple eyes are on their backs.

Dragonflies have the largest eyes of any insect. Each of their compound eyes has 30,000 lenses.

Feet that taste things

Bugs taste things by walking on them, using their feet or taste sensors on their legs.

Bees can tell how sweet nectar is just by standing on the flower.

Flies can taste an apple as soon as they land on it.

Some other insects taste things with their wings.

Noisy bugs

Bugs make sounds to attract mates or warn off their enemies. Some do this by rubbing their legs together.

The loudest insects are Cicadas.

Some insects can use sound to confuse their enemies. Tiger Moths can use ultrasonic clicks that jam the tracking sonar of the Brown Bats that feed on them.

Bug ears

You could say that hearing is an insect invention. They were the first animals in the world that were able to make sounds and hear them. But very few insects have ears in their heads.

When insects first evolved 400 million years ago, all of them were deaf. Almost all of the Beetles are still deaf. Some other insect species have developed many different ways of hearing. Some are able to hear sounds that are far beyond what humans can hear.

Crickets and Katydids hear with their knees

The males of these two species always sing the loudest. They do it by rubbing a ridge on one of their wings against a row of teeth on the other wing. The females hear the males' songs through ears on their front legs.

Grasshoppers, Cicadas and Locusts have their hearing organs on their abdomens. Grasshoppers have the most ears, with six pairs of them along the sides of their abdomens. Praying Mantises have just one super-ear in the middle of their chests. For some Flies, the hearing sensor is in their necks.

Bugs have no lungs

Bugs breathe, but they do it without having any lungs. Instead, they have tubes and air sacs. These pump air through their bodies and deliver oxygen where it's needed. They don't breathe through their noses.

Fun Bug Facts for Kids

Bugs use their antennae to sense and feel their way around.

Insects have air openings, called spiracles, lining the sides of their abdomens. They're belly breathing!

This system works for bugs, but it also means they have to stay small. In order for them to get bigger, we'd need to have an atmosphere that has more oxygen in the air. If our world suddenly changed to have more oxygen in the air, one thing that would happen is that bugs would get bigger.

Feeling the air

Most insects have hairs that aren't there to keep them warm. Instead, these sensitive hairs measure how fast the air is moving. Bugs that live in water use their hair detectors to judge movements in the water.

Bugs' antennae are recycled legs

Insects evolved from creatures that had many legs and many body segments, or sections. Over time, the extra legs they no longer needed became mouth parts or antennae. Some of the body parts fused together. The front ones became their heads.

Noisy bugs

Some bugs make sounds to talk to each other using vibrations. One is the Madagascar Hissing Cockroach. It uses its spiracles, or breathing holes along its abdomen, to make hissing noises. It hopes these noises will scare away its enemies by warning that it could attack.

Death's Head Hawkmoths make a squeaky noise by pushing air out of their bodies to scare off worker Honeybees.

Cicadas are the loudest noise maker bugs

Male Cicadas are louder than the females. The males have sound boxes in their abdomens. Inside their abdomens is a tymbal, or sound box. They make their songs by making the tymbal larger and smaller. They do it to attract female Cicadas, who answer with clicking noises. The hotter the day is, the louder the male Cicadas get in singing their love songs.

Some bugs rely on clever camo, like this Leaf Bug.

Scents sense

Bugs use the smells they make to talk to each other. Their smells work to attract mates, to tell others of their species it's time for a get together, to mark a trail and to repel enemies.

Smell signals work differently than body language or sound signals. Smell signals travel on the air, sometimes for long distances and don't fade away quickly.

The males of some Moth species can travel almost 30 miles, or 48 kilometres, following the scent of a signaling female. Honeybee queens send a scent signal that gives their orders to all the worker Bees in the hive.

Most Butterflies have claws on their front legs, but Fritillary Butterflies, like this one, don't. Fritillarys eat flower nectar from thistles, coneflowers, joy-pye weed, ironweed and violets. They live in Southern United States, Mexico, Central America, South America and the Caribbean countries.

How do bugs defend themselves?

Some bugs are brightly colored, not to look good to humans but to look scary or warn other creatures that might eat them. Their colors are a signal that they are toxic or poisonous if attacked or eaten.

Other ways bugs defend themselves are by using sounds, stingers or camouflage. Stick Insects pretend to be sticks and hope that predators can't see them.

Other bugs pretend to be a bug species they aren't. Bees and Wasps use this strategy.

Some Beetles can spray poisons from their abdomens, a form of chemical warfare. Not only can they shoot with their bellies, they can aim at their predators with surprising accuracy!

A lot of bugs can fly

Only three animals on earth today can fly. They are:

- all bats
- most birds
- some insects.

There are some other animals that can glide for short distances like flying fish and some Asian snakes that can glide from tree to tree, but only these three animals are the world's true fliers. It was the insects who flew first.

For their first million years on earth bugs couldn't fly. Then they worked out how to do it and discovered what a useful skill it is. Being able to fly means they can move faster, over greater distances, to find food, new places to live or mates or to escape their enemies.

Some modern bugs can't fly, like Silverfish. Or most Ants. Or some Beetles.

Bugs that have wings usually have two pairs of wings, not just one. Beetles have two pairs of wings, but their outer wings are hard and don't work for flying.

Some bugs with big wings, like Antlions, aren't very good fliers. Some with small wings, like bees and wasps, are. Some are clumsy fliers, like some Beetles and True Bugs. The Dragonflies and True Flies are aerial acrobats.

The fastest bug fliers are Sphinx Moths. They can fly up to 33 miles per hour, or 53 kilometres per hour.

The highest any bug has ever been seen flying is Butterflies, as high as 20,000 feet or 6,100 metres above the ground.

Bugs that swim

Many insects live underwater for part of their lives. Some have developed unique ways of moving underwater. All the Water Beetles have paddles on their legs.

Dragonfly nymphs or larva get around even faster using jet propulsion. They do it by forcing water out of their rear ends.

Water Scorpions are bugs, even though they're called scorpions. They have breathing tubes on their behinds. This allows them to breathe when they're hanging upside down in the water. It also means they can hunt near the surface of polluted ponds that have almost no oxygen.

Fun Bug Facts for Kids

This Bee gets covered in pollen when it visits a flower for sweet nectar. Then it takes the pollen to other flowers, pollinating the plants. The Bee gets nectar and the flower gets to make new plants, so they both win!

Bugs that walk on water

Water Striders can walk on water, with the ends of their legs barely touching the surface. They can detect even the slightest ripples on the water and rush to that spot to devour the insect that made the ripples.

On their nectar and pollen collecting journeys, a Bee can fly 60 miles, or 96.5 kilometres in a single day.

Are bugs smart?

A lot of people, including most scientists, used to think that any animal with a small head must have a small brain. Small, they reasoned, means not very smart. True, creatures with small brains could find food, shelter and mates and avoid their enemies, but that's about all they could do. Or so we thought. But old ideas about animals are changing as more species are being studied more closely, including insects.

We know surprisingly little about the insect world, given how long humans and bugs have lived together on earth. The most-studied bug species are Ants and Bees. Both are smart in surprising ways. Ants can send signals to each other to help them attack a predator or a threat as a group. We're still not sure how they do it.

Bees can be trained to recognize a human face if it's the one that gives them a sweet treat.

Bees can learn paths to the best flowers. They can tell other Bees exactly where to find those flowers. Bees are also able to solve other problems, even though their brains are only about the size of a poppy seed.

They can size up their flower options, only going for the best nectar and pollen. The amount and quality of nectar and pollen constantly changes in flowers hour by hour, so this is more difficult than it sounds. Bees can make quick decisions and memorize their territories. They are able to learn. And it's possible

A pair of ladybugs.

that when they sleep, they dream. There's no proof of this yet. What is proven is that Bees can count.

They can also remember. Bees learn not by trial and error, but by watching other Bees do a task. This is another sign of intelligence.

Bees might even be what scientists call "self-aware." This means that, like humans, and what we used to think was a very short list of animals, Bees are individuals.

They think and have feelings. They have emotions. They can suffer anxiety, as well as pain. This might be true of many other insect species.

They just haven't been studied yet so we don't know how much bug smarts bugs have.

Where do bugs go in winter?

Most bugs live short lives. In their adult stage, they may only live for part of one day or only a few weeks. Bugs have three ways of making sure that their kind survives through the coldest months of the year.

A few species migrate to warmer places, returning in spring. Others move underground, or they hibernate.

Some shelter in hollow trees, or under piles of fallen leaves. Some insects are able to replace the water in their bodies with glycerol, a bug antifreeze!

The nymphs of Mayflies, Dragonflies and Stone Flies can live under the ice in ponds and streams. Silkworms spend the winter in their pupa stage, cozy and warm in their own cocoons. The Praying Mantis's cold weather strategy is to lay eggs that can survive the cold and hatch in Spring.

Some insects hibernate as adults. This includes Lady Bugs, Wasps and Honeybees. They can slow their bodies down to almost a stop and sleep deeply, living off their stored energy for months until warm weather returns.

The last time anyone saw a Xerces Blue Butterfly was back in 1941. Their last habitat was the coast and dunes near San Francisco, California. Their habitat was lost as the city grew larger. The Xerces Blue was the first Butterfly in North America to become extinct because of humans.

Bug babies

Most insects lay eggs, but a few, like some Cockroaches, are born alive.

The eggs of some, like Aphids and Tsetse flies, hatch as soon as they are laid.

Most insect eggs are drought-resistant.

Most bugs are bad parents

Some bugs are good parents, but most of them aren't. The mothers lay their eggs and leave. The fathers don't do anything for their bug kids.

But a few of the True Bugs, the ones scientists call Hemiptera (say this: HEM-ip-tear-ah), do look after their babies. Some hide their eggs. Some put a toxin in their eggs that doesn't hurt them but does hurt any other animal that eats the eggs. Others provide food for their young.

There is one bug dad that helps with the baby bug care. The Giant Water Bug female lays her eggs on the wings of her mate. Then he does all the caring for them until they hatch.

The longest bug migration that we know of is Painted Lady Butterflies. Each year they fly from North Africa to Iceland, a distance of 6,437 kilometres or 4,000 miles.

These are larvae of Monarch Butterflies.

Metamorphosis

Most insects have either 3 or 4 life stages from egg to adult. This is called metamorphosis.

Grasshoppers are a 3-stage insect, going from egg to nymph to adult. In 3-stage metamorphosis, the nymph usually looks like a smaller adult, though it might be a different color.

Butterflies are 4-stage insects, going from egg to larva to pupa to adult. In 4-stage metamorphosis, the animal's body changes completely with each new stage of its life. The larva stage is a caterpillar. The pupa stage looks like a beetle, wrapped in its cocoon. It emerges with wet wings, waits for them to dry, and soon after that the new adult mates.

The feet of a Housefly are 10 million times more sensitive to the taste of sugar than a human tongue.

Flies

All Flies have two wings and halterers just behind their wings. Halterers are organs that help them balance when they're flying.

The larvae of all Flies are called maggots. They have gills or breathing tubes and live in water or in damp places, like anything that is rotting.

Some Flies are amazing mimics, looking and acting just like their prey. There are Bee Flies, Flower Flies and Robber Flies. Bee Flies and Flower Flies look like bees. The Flower Flies are larger and look more like Bumble Bees. Unlike real Bees, these Flower Flies can't make honey and don't live in hives.

Robber Flies are also called Assassin Flies because they're skilled ambush hunters, attacking other Flies at night.

One type of Fly, the Midge, can beat its wings 1,048 times per second. It easily beats the fastest bird in this category, the hummingbird. Hummers beat their wings at only 70 beats per second.

All Flies like heat and light.

Though we know Flies as biters, they also help us. Flies are pollinators. Their maggots eat Aphids, Moth caterpillars and Beetle grubs. For their pest insect-eating abilities, some types of Flies are used for natural pest control.

Scientists who study bugs are called entomologists. (say this: ENT-toe-mall-oh-jists).

There have been Houseflies like this one for far longer than there have been humans for them to pester. Houseflies evolved about 50 million years ago.

Houseflies and horseflies

Housefly adults only live for about a month. In that time the females lay between 500 and 2,000 eggs. If you had just one mating pair of Houseflies in your home in April and they could find plenty of food, and if all their babies survived and kept mating, by August there would be

191,000,000,000,000,000,000 Houseflies living at your place!

Besides all the noise your new guests would make, you'd probably be worried about your health. Housefly stings carry bacteria and viruses and can cause conjunctivitis, dysentery, typhoid fever and yaws in humans.

Ticks and Fleas

Ticks and Fleas can't fly. Both are mammal bloodsuckers, but Fleas are much smaller than Ticks. Fleas can leap up to 350 times the length of their own bodies. Deer Ticks are the ones whose bites can spread Lyme Disease.

Dust mites

If you think you sleep alone, you're wrong! The average bed in an American home contains between 2 million and 6 million Dust Mites. These Mites eat dead human skin cells and need warm, humid places to live. They are far too small to see, but for people who are allergic to them, Dust Mites can cause big problems with breathing.

A Dust mite allergy is a trigger for asthma attacks. These Mites can live in carpets, curtains and upholstered furniture as well as bed mattresses and bedsheets, covers or duvets.

Fireflies

Fireflies have bellies that light up at night. They aren't Flies, they're Beetles. They are bioluminescent (say this: BYE-yo-loom-in-ESS-ent). This means they can use light flashes to attract their mates or attract their prey. The colors they flash can be blue, green or red. You are most likely to see them doing this in your backyard or in parks or meadows on summer evenings. Other names for Fireflies are Lightning Bugs and Glowworms.

Their itchy bites are usually harmless, but some Mosquito bites cause the people they bite to get malaria or yellow fever. Worldwide, diseases carried by Mosquitos kill about 2 million people every year.

Mosquitos

Mosquitos feed on flower nectar and fruits. They hear with their antennae. Tiny hairs on their wings can sense air flow.

Mosquitos are attracted to the heat of a mammal's skin. They see this heat using their infrared vision. They are also attracted to body smells, such as human's sweaty feet, the carbon dioxide we exhale with each breath or flowery smelling shampoos or body lotions we use.

An egg will hatch and the Mosquito will grow to become an adult in just 4 to 7 days. They live their entire lives within 1 mile, or 1.6 kilometers, of where they were born.

Only female mosquitos bite because they need to feed on mammal blood to be able to make their eggs.

Sundew plants eat insects, including Mosquitos. Sundews usually grow in warm countries including Australia, South Africa and in South America, however there is a type of Sundew that thrives in Scotland!

Some people use citronella-scented candles to chase Mosquitos away from their decks or patios in summer. Citronella works to repel Mosquitos not because these bugs don't care for the smell, but because citronella damages their feet.

Lice

Lice are tiny bugs with no wings. They live on blood. Head Lice live in human hair and bite people's heads and shoulders. Their favorite humans to bite are women and children. They spread easily between people, but less often to pets. They can live in clothing or bed covers and sheets but need to feed often to survive.

A strange thing about Lice is they like to bite boys less than girls. Another odd thing about Lice is they bite all races and ethnic groups, but they mostly avoid people with an African American heritage. Scientists have some theories about this, but haven't proven why.

Bedbugs

Bedbugs are tiny. They're only as big as the head of a pin. They're brown, oval and could be hiding in your bedroom. They can't fly, but they can lay hundreds of eggs. A female Bedbug lays eggs every day of her adult life.

They hide during the day and only come out at night, drawn by the carbon dioxide exhaled by sleeping humans. You probably won't even realize you have Bedbugs at home or have slept at a hotel with Bedbugs until you see the red, itchy rash they cause on your body.

Like Ticks, Bedbugs are hard to see.

Ticks only bite once, but Bedbugs are repeat biters. They are hard to get rid of because they're resistant to insecticides. They can travel easily in clothing and in the suitcases of people on vacation.

Bedbugs are one of the animals that is increasing, and spreading, with climate change. In cold weather, they are able to go into hibernation, and stay that way for as long as 450 days!

Bedbugs' hibernating skills are so impressive that NASA has funded a study to see if it would be possible for humans travelling to distant planets to go into a long but healthy deep sleep, just like the Bedbugs already know how to do, until the human space explorers reach their far-away destinations.

Insects are the only animals without a backbone that can fly.

Cockroaches

Cockroaches are another bad bug that people put a lot of work into getting rid of. Cockroaches aren't picky eaters. They eat just about anything, but their favorite food is the glue on postage stamps and envelopes. They can survive a month without food, but just a week without water.

A Cockroach that loses its head will stay alive until if finally dies of starvation.

A female Cockroach can have 2,000,000 babies each year. Some species of Roaches have pouches, like kangaroos, to carry their babies.

Cockroaches are skilled at getting into small spaces. They can squeeze into a place just a quarter as high as they are. They're also fast runners, with the fastest roaches (they live in the tropics) moving more than 50 times their own length per second! That would be the same as a human adult who could run at 322 kilometres or 200 miles per hour!

Cockroach abilities have inspired researchers at University of California Berkeley to create a 6-legged emergency aid robot that has Cockroach speed and agility. Like Roaches, this robot can recoil its legs. The robot needs to be able to make itself smaller to get through rubble to search for survivors after bombings or natural disasters.

The world's birds eat between 400 and 500 million tons (or 363 to 454 tonnes) of insects every year.

Aphids can completely take over and destroy a plant in just a few days.

Aphids

Almost all Aphids are female. Aphids don't lay eggs. They are born as nymphs and most of them are already pregnant. When the plant they live on gets too crowded with other Aphids, or the plant is sick or dying, some Aphid species are able to change their bodies so that their next baby nymphs are born with wings to fly to another, healthy host plant.

Ladybugs are brilliant Aphid-eaters, used as a natural way to get rid of them without having to use poisonous insecticides which can also harm or kill good bugs.

Lacewing

They live everywhere in the world that is warm, except desserts. But you probably won't see the adults, because they hide themselves during the day and are active at night.

Like many flying insects, Lacewings lay their eggs on the undersides of leaves.

Caterpillars have 12 eyes, 6 on each side of their heads. But even with all these eyes, everything looks blurry to them and they can't see shapes. All they can see is if it's light or dark out.

Honeybees tending their hive.

Meet the pollinators

Bees are the most famous pollinator insect species, but there are other insect pollinators including Flies, Beetles, Hoverflies, Monarch Butterflies, Wasps and some Moths. A non-bug pollinator is hummingbirds.

A third of all the food humans eat is pollinated by insects. 80% of our food crops depend on bugs doing this job for us. If we woke up tomorrow and all the pollinating insects had mysteriously vanished, humans would probably become extinct on Earth. If all the humans and animals on Earth suddenly vanished, the insects would survive as long as there were still plants.

Social bugs

Some insects are social. They live in communities where each bug has a job to do for their bug community to survive. These can be more complex, more co-operative, and more organized than any human community.

For this reason, their colonies or hives are sometimes called superorganisms. This means that several animals, thousands or even millions, behave together as if they are one super animal.

Bees, Ants, Termites, and some Wasps are all social insects. In order to make their bug cities work, they have developed ways to communicate with each other even though they don't use words, as humans do.

Bees

124 million years ago, there were no Bees as we know them. Until then, all the Bees were still Wasps. The first Bees evolved from Wasps. For the first 60 million or so years, they lived alone, not in hives. There are still many species of Bees that don't live in hives.

Bees evolved along with flowers.

The first Bees were very small because at that time flowers were small.

Bees can see ultraviolet light and polarized light, helping them find flowers brimming with nectar and pollen. Just by standing on a flower they can tell how sweet its nectar is.

For the Bee species that do live in hives, most of their babies are females because all of the hive workers are female. So are all the scouting Bees and collector Bees. The very few male bees only exist to mate with the hive's queen.

Most Bee species are black and yellow, but Orchid Bees have brilliant iridescent colors of blue, red and green. It is the males of this species that visit the orchid flowers.

Beekeeping began about 9,000 years ago, probably in northern Africa.

Bees are surprisingly smart. They can count. Researchers using food rewards have even taught some Bees to play soccer.

A worker Bee collects nectar for her hive.

Honey Bees

Honeybees are the only Bees to leave their stingers in the wound when they sting. Because stinging means they lose their stingers, they die. Worker Bees do all the work and so it might be true that they die of exhaustion. They only live for 6 to 8 weeks.

It is the worker Bees who decide when to make a new queen.

This happens when their queen is too old to lay eggs, or she leaves the hive, or she dies. To make a new queen, the workers build longer cells around a few eggs and feed them royal jelly. It's a mixture of water, sugars and a protein the workers secrete from their heads.

Royal jelly doesn't include any pollen or honey. All Bee eggs get a little bit of Royal jelly at first, but only the new queens get fed nothing but royal jelly until they are adults. A new queen will emerge 16 days later and attack any other queens who haven't hatched yet.

When there are two or more queen Bees born in a hive, queens will walk through the hive piping. That means making a sound, something like quacking. Piping tells the workers it's time to defend their favorite queen. When the queens meet, they will fight until the strongest one wins and all the other queens are dead. The winner of this Game of Queens mates with one of the few male Bees each hive has. Sometimes, when there are two queens, one will leave with her workers to form a new hive somewhere else.

A queen Honeybee can lay 2,500 eggs in one day.

Honeybees need to visit 2 million flowers and make 10 million trips back and forth to their hive to collect enough nectar to make 1 pound or .45 kilogram of honey. Collector Bees have a nectar pouch that is separate from their stomach.

Honeybees do a complicated dance to tell each other where the best flowers are. This is called Bee dance language. They tell direction by the angle to the sun a Bee must travel to find the exact flower they're describing. How long the dance lasts tells other Bees how far away that flower is.

A Honeybee would have enough energy to fly around the world if it ate 1 ounce, or just over 28 grams of honey.

Bees make honey for themselves and resent sharing it with other hungry animals or humans. Almost all honey is a healthy food for people. The exception is Mad Honey. It looks reddish rather than golden. It tastes a bit bitter. And it can be dangerous if you eat it, causing your heartrate to slow down and hallucinations. You might also be paralyzed. Fortunately, all of these effects are only temporary. If you accidentally ate some Mad Honey, you'd be fine by the next day.

Bees don't make Mad Honey to hurt humans stealing honey from their nests. It happens naturally when the Bees visit rhododendron flowers. Rhododendrons grow in many places in the world from the Arctic to the tropics, including in United States. Honey that you buy from beekeepers or in a store or farmers market is totally safe. Wild honey you take from a hive you find might not be.

Humans have known about mad honey for thousands of years.

Ancient armies of the Greeks and Romans used mad honey, leaving it out for enemy soldiers to find. It was easier to confuse and defeat hungry soldiers tricked into eating the mad honey.

Africanized Honeybees or Killer Bees

European Bees that were taken to Africa quickly evolved to be more aggressive, fiercely defending their hives from humans who tried to steal their honey.

Then, in 1956, a Brazilian researcher wanted to breed Bees that would produce more honey and be more able to thrive in tropical countries. Encouraged by honey producers, he crossbred Honeybees and hardy African Bees. The result was a success. These new Bees proved to be stronger and more resilient to disease. But they're also far more aggressive. These are Bees with attitude!

Then this new scientific breakthrough went very wrong. Some of these new, angry Bees escaped in 1957. They had no problem surviving in the wild. They thrived, soon outcompeting the native Bees for food.

Africanized Bees are better at harvesting pollen and they work harder and have more babies than the milder European Bees. They also don't want to work to feed anyone except themselves, making them much harder for beekeepers to manage. And downright dangerous to people, who they chase and sting repeatedly.

More than 1,000 Americans have died after getting multiple bee stings.

These Bees have now spread north through northern South America to Central America, most of Mexico and into southern United States, from Texas to California, and they are still on the move. It is only colder winters in northern United States and Canada that has kept Africanized Bees from moving even further north. As our climate warms, these Bees will surely continue their march north to conquer new homes and threaten both the native Bees and people who live there.

Wasps

A Wasp's stinger is also a drill, an egg-laying tube and a venom injector.

The first Wasps on earth were vegetarian, eating only plants. They had no sting. None of them would evolve to sting until about 190 million years ago.

Some Wasps today are still vegetarian, living entirely on pollen. Others hunt and eat other insects including Wasps and Bees.

All Wasps love sweets, especially honey or rotting fruit.

If you have an apple tree and leave fallen apples on the ground, they will soon be covered in Wasps.

All Wasps have an excellent sense of smell. The smells they hate are peppermint, spearmint, basil, cloves, geraniums, thyme, bay leaves, citronella and lemongrass. They also don't like vinegar, cinnamon, coffee grounds and sliced cucumbers.

These are Paper Wasps. Paper was invented almost 2,000 years ago, inspired by the hanging hives of Paper Wasps.

Some orchids have a clever way of using Wasps to pollinate them. The plants mimic the look and smell of a female Wasp. Male Wasps swoon, helplessly in love, stumbling from flower to flower and spreading the orchid's pollen.

Fig Wasps

Figs depend on Fig Wasps. If there are no Fig Wasps, there will be no figs. They evolved their relationship with figs about 70 to 90 million years ago.

This is a Ruby-tailed or Cuckoo Wasp, a type of parasite Wasp.

Wasps that are parasites

Scientists believe there could be as many as 1 million species of Parasite Wasps, though only 100,000 of these tiny Wasp species have been identified so far.

Parasites are animals that live on, or in, another animal or human. They harm their host or kill them. Bed bugs, Fleas and Lice are all parasites, and so are Mosquitos.

Parasitoid Wasps lay their eggs inside another insect. When the eggs hatch, the babies eat that insect.

Some Parasitoid Wasps are helpful to humans. These Wasps inject their eggs into Aphids or other insects that are attacking food crops like vegetables grown in greenhouses or wheat growing in fields.

Some farmers have found using the Wasps works better and is cheaper than using pesticides to kill the pest insects attacking their crops.

Using insects to control insects is also better for the environment.

Gall Wasps

Gall Wasps have a strange talent. They have learned how to make some plants protect their babies. When a Gall Wasp lays her eggs on the underside of a Southern Beech or Oak tree leaf, or on a Rose leaf, the plant grows a protective coat around the eggs, called a gall.

Fairy Wasp or Fairy Fly

The Fairy Fly is a species of Parasite Wasp. It is the world's smallest insect, only .14 millimeter or .005 inch long. You would need a high-powered microscope to be able to see one.

A Fairy Wasp spends most of its life inside its host insect, the Bark Wasp. The adults have short lives, only living for a few days.

Wasps use their venom for both hunting and defense.

Cicada Killer Wasps

If the Cicadas are coming to your town, you might want to draft in some Cicada Killer Wasps. They're large and fierce looking wasps that are 2 inches, or 5 centimetres long. They appear in summer and live in most of United States. Their lives are short, just 8 weeks, and their nests are underground.

A female will make a burrow, then attack a flying Cicada, paralyzing it in flight with her sting. Then they glide together in the direction of the Cicada Killer Wasp's burrow. She lays one egg and seals it up in the burrow with 1, 2 or sometimes 3 captive Cicadas for the larva to eat when it hatches.

The mother lays several eggs, each in its own burrow room with its own Cicadas to eat and brings more food each day for about two weeks. That's when the larvae each spin a cocoon of their own silk mixed with sand or soil.

The mother leaves, her parenting duties done. Her larvae are now all pupas who will remain in their cocoons all winter. They'll emerge the next summer as adults.

Emerald Jewel Wasp

A female Emerald Jewel Wasp will give two stings to a much larger Cockroach. The first sting temporarily paralyzes the roaches' front legs. The second sting is directly to one part of the Cockroach's brain that makes the Cockroach a zombie slave to the Wasp. Then the Wasp uses the Cockroach's antennae as a leash and leads it to her underground lair where it will become living but helpless food for her babies.

Hornets

Hornets can be scary looking, especially the Northern Giant Hornet, native to Asia but an invasive species in the Pacific Northwest and coastal British Columbia. They were first spotted there in 2019, and soon got the name Murder Hornets. People became so riled up about them that some people started killing bees, wasps and just about any insect they spotted. Hornet hysteria took over for a while.

Fun Bug Facts for Kids

All Hornets are meat-eaters. They live in ground dens that can have 400,000 to 500,000 Hornets.

Northern Giants are big, for a Hornet. They are 1.5 inches, or 3.8 centimeters long! That makes them the world's largest Wasp. They sting over and over. Their stings can be fatal.

Hornets aren't a separate species.

They are an especially aggressive type of Wasp, with a much more painful sting. They attack other insects, mainly Honeybees, cutting off the Bees' heads and stealing their honey. A Northern Giant Hornet can kill 40 Honeybees in just 1 minute! The Bees fight back by flapping their wings so hard it raises the temperature to 40 degrees Centigrade, or 104 degrees Fahrenheit. Hornets can't take the heat and they die.

One out of every 4 animals on earth is a Beetle. Beetles don't have any ears. Most of them are deaf. The Beetle on the left is a European Stripe Bug. The one on the right looks like a scorpion, but that's just for scaring off predators. It's actually a Devil's Coach Horse Beetle.

Beetles

Feather-winged Beetles are so tiny you can hardly see them. Some tropical Beetles are so big, they're the size of an adult man's hand!

Most Beetles only live for 1 year. They can't see very well and most of them are deaf. Instead, they use smells, sounds or vibrations in the ground to understand their world, find food or mates and avoid their enemies.

Ladybugs, Fireflies, Waterstriders and Lightning Bugs are all Beetles.

Fun Bug Facts for Kids

Some Beetles are plant-eaters, others are hunters or scavengers of other animals and a few are parasites. Most live on land, but some live in the water and are good swimmers.

They live almost everywhere on earth, from deserts to forests, cities to the countryside and even on or near mountain tops!

There is one type of Beetle that farms its own food!

The tropical Ambrosia Beetle digs holes in old tree trunks to grow a type of fungus that is their favorite food. Scientists who tried to grow the same fungus in a laboratory kept having a problem with mold attacking their fungi. It seems the Ambrosia Beetles have a way of getting rid of this mold. Researchers are still trying to understand how they do it.

It is Beetles that do the work of breaking down dead stuff in forests. They are also destructive, killing trees and attacking food crops in the fields or stored meats, milk, flour, cereals, nuts, fruits and grains needed to feed people and animals.

Titan Beetles are the largest known Beetles. They can grow to be 7 inches, or almost 18 centimeters long. Their bite is strong enough to snap a pencil in two.

Honeybees need to visit 2 million flowers and fly 80,000 kilometres, or 49,709 miles, to make one pound or half a kilogram of honey. That distance is the same as flying around the world twice.

Doodlebugs

Doodlebugs are the larvae of the Antlion. In the larva stage, it is a Beetle. As an adult, it looks like a Dragonfly, with very long, see-through wings.

Antlions don't stalk their prey. Instead, they set a trap.

They do this by digging a round pit in dry sand or soil. This pit has very steep sides. The Antlion lurks at the bottom of the pit, buried with only its open jaws showing. An Ant that stumbles into the pit is doomed. It will struggle to escape until finally, exhausted, it falls into the jaws waiting below.

Antlions don't need to drink water. They get all the moisture they need from their prey.

They can survive in the desert when it is 40 degrees C., or 104 degrees F., far too hot for most animals.

Ladybugs or Ladybirds

Ladybugs live on every continent on Earth. They hibernate in winter in huge colonies in rotten logs, under rocks or sometimes in the walls of houses.

Not all Ladybugs are female. Some are male, but they're still called Ladybugs. A Ladybug can eat more than 5,000 Aphids in her or his lifetime.

Ladybugs shoot a smelly liquid at predators to defend themselves. This liquid comes from their knees.

Ladybugs come in different colors and some have stripes, but the most familiar one looks like this one. It's red or orange with 7 black spots. They aren't natives in North America. They came here from Europe.

Stink bugs

Stink bugs don't sting, bite or damage buildings like some bugs can, but they are considered pests for two reasons. The first one is they eat food crops. The second is they smell really bad.

Stink bugs don't make their bad smells by farting. Instead, they make their stinks by making a chemical in glands on the sides of their bodies. They release this chemical to scare off their predators.

An Asian native, they now live in other places in the world including United States. In winter, they look for places to hibernate, including in people's homes. If you try to kill them by sweeping them up or vacuuming them, they release their nasty stink!

Dragonflies

Most insects can fly, but Dragonflies are one of the fastest fliers in the insect world. They can do this because of their air sacs and massive muscles in their thorax. Their powerful flight muscles use a lot of oxygen.

A Dragonfly nymph, that's the baby, lives entirely underwater until it is 5 years old. In that time, it will need to molt 15 times as it grows.

Dragonflies are exceptional hunters. They are able to catch their prey 9 times out of every 10 attempts.

Most Dragonfly species live in the tropics.

Like many cities in North America, the City of Edmonton, in Alberta, Canada, usually spends half a million dollars each summer on pesticide sprays to control Mosquitoes. In 2022, they used Dragonflies instead, and it worked. Not only did the city save money, but it was also a more eco-friendly way to control pesky Mosquitos.

Most insects die soon after they become adults. For some, their adult life lasts only hours.

Dragonflies are precision fliers. With two sets of wings, they can perform air acrobatics and can land upside down on a leaf.

Katydids

Katydids are sometimes called Bush Crickets or Long-horned Grasshoppers. They have the smallest ears of any animal. They have one ear on each leg, just below their knees.

Katydids can hear the ultrasonic clicks that hunting bats make, helping the Katydids to avoid them.

As adults, Katydids have green bodies. They look a lot like Grasshoppers. The largest Katydids can be 5 inches, or almost 13 centimetres long. They usually sleep during the day and are awake at night.

They can also mimic the songs of female Cicadas. This attracts male Cicadas who want to mate. The lovelorn Cicadas are tricked into coming close enough that the waiting Katydids can strike and eat them.

Praying Mantises have only one ear. It's in the middle of their chests.

Praying mantis

A Praying Mantis male dies for love. In most types of Praying Mantises when they're mating the female may start eating her mate. She starts with his head and keeps on munching, but he doesn't let that distract him. By the time they're done mating, only his abdomen is left.

Praying Mantises can turn their heads nearly all the way around to look back over their shoulders.

They attack animals much larger than they are, including frogs, mice, lizards and small birds. They also eat spiders, Bees and Beetles.

Fun Bug Facts for Kids

To human ears, the sound Crickets make is chirping. What we can't hear without help from electronics is that Crickets sing songs to each other. These songs can be as complex as birdsong.

Crickets

If you want to know what their songs sound like, get some crickets and a microphone and record them. Then hit playback through speakers and turn up the volume. What you'll hear is the many and varied mating songs of Crickets.

Their songs depend on how warm it is out on a summer day. The cooler it is out, the lower and slower their song will be.

Mexican Jumping Beans jump because there is a Bean Moth caterpillar inside.

The male Cicada is the world's loudest known insect. Its mating song can be heard from 440 yards or 402 meters away.

Cicada Explosion

Big Bug Newsflash: In the summer of 2024 there's going to be an explosion of Cicadas in United States (or if it's after summer 2024, it's already happened).

This natural wonder hasn't happened since 1803. It won't happen again until 2245. We are incredibly fortunate that we'll be able to see it in our lifetime!

But people in the Midwest and Southern United States might not agree about how wondrous a Cicada explosion is when millions of Cicadas come up out of the earth and start making their loud buzzing sounds.

Fun Bug Facts for Kids

They'll begin to appear in late April. Then, for about 6 weeks, things are going to get loud! Really loud.

A gang of Cicadas can make as much noise as a jet taking off!

Estimates are there are going to be about 1 trillion Cicadas. Each one is just over an inch, or 2.5 centimeters long. If you laid them all end to end, they could reach from earth to the moon and back again 33 times!

Here's how this happens. In United States, there are many groups of Cicadas. These groups are called Broods. Each brood has a life cycle of living for several years underground, only coming back to the surface to mate every so many years. It is very rare for two broods to emerge in the same year, but that's what will be big news in 2024. Brood 19 only shows up every 13 years. Brood 13 only does it every 17 years. For both of them, 2024 is their year.

It is only every 221 years that BOTH broods tunnel their way up out of the ground and emerge.

First they molt. Then the males buzz, really loudly, to find their mates.

While lots of people might want to avoid the Cicadas Explosion of 2024, scientists will be coming from around the world to study it. But if you live in the Midwest or the Southeast, you won't just have a front row seat, you'll be in the middle of the show!

Cicadas don't bite or sting. They are useful bugs because their tunnels help get water down to plant roots and they are food for birds. They mate, lay their eggs and die in stinky piles. If this happens where you live, the dead bugs are excellent and free fertilizer for your garden plants.

Silkworms

It takes 2,000 Silkworm cocoons to make 1 pound of silk.

A Silkworm is not a worm. It's the larva, or caterpillar, of a Silk Moth. Silkworms eat nothing but mulberry leaves. When it is ready to transform into a Silk Moth, the caterpillar will spin silk to make its cocoon.

Each Silkworm can spin a single silk thread that is 900 metres, or 980 yards long.

It takes between 2,000 and 5,000 Silkworm cocoons to make just one pound or almost half a kilogram of silk.

Silk cloth and clothing was first made in China about 5,000 years ago.

Today, Silkworms are grown for silk making and for food in Korea, China and Japan. They are extinct as wild animals, so are now entirely servants to serve humans. To make silk, the cocoons are boiled, then unraveled. The pupae inside the cocoons are sold as a street food snack in Korea, or used in rice dishes in China. In Japan, Silkworms are sometimes used for fishing bait.

There are 17,500 species of Butterflies in the world that we've found so far, but only 750 of them live in United States. This is an adult Glasswing Butterfly. A South American native, the furthest north that Glasswings live is in Texas.

Female Silk Moths have small mouths, but they never eat. They lay their eggs on mulberry leaves and die. Though they have wings, Silk Moths can't fly.

Butterflies

Butterflies got their name in a strange way. There was a legend that witches could turn themselves into flying bugs to go and search for food. The food these witches wanted the most was butter. The bugs that helped them find it became known as Butterflies.

Butterflies lay their eggs and glue them to the undersides of leaves. They choose the plants that baby caterpillars will munch on after they hatch.

Adult Butterflies can't bite or chew their food. They need to slurp up nectar sap and juice from rotting fruits. They do this using their proboscis (say this: pro-BOSS-sus). It's shaped like a straw.

Butterflies' ears are on their wings.

They tune their ears to the same sound frequencies as the birds that eat them. The Butterflies listen for wing beats, territorial birdcalls, bird feet hopping and bird feathers swooshing.

Monarch Butterflies are probably the best-known Butterfly in United States, partly because of their brilliant colors but also for their long annual migrations. But they aren't the only Butterflies that migrate. The Painted Lady, Purple Wing, Great Southern White, Cloudless Sulphur and Little Sulphur as well as the Buckeye Butterfly are also migrators.

Count the number of times a Field Cricket chirps in 15 seconds. Add 40 to the total and this will tell you what the temperature is in Fahrenheit, or degrees F. Or count the number of chirps for 8 seconds and add 5 to tell the temperature in degrees Celsius.

Monarch Butterflies are very endangered. Since the 1990s, there are 90% fewer of them in Eastern United States.

Monarch Butterfly

As summer ends and the weather cools in southern Canada and northern United States, millions of Monarch Butterflies travel to spend the winter in the fir and pine forests west of Mexico City in Mexico. There, they huddle together in masses to keep warm. As spring arrives, the Monarch Butterflies travel back to their northern homes.

Their long migration is as far as 3,000 miles, or 4,828 kilometres, each way.

This trip is so long and so dangerous that no single Butterfly ever makes the entire trip south and back north again.

There is also a small group of Monarchs that spend their winters on California's coast, then return to their homes, west of the Rocky Mountains.

The threats to Monarchs include farmers who use pesticides on their fields to kill insects or herbicides to kill weeds, homeowners using pesticides and herbicides on their lawns and gardens and illegal logging in Mexico.

The only thing the yellow, black and cream Monarch caterpillars eat is the milkweed plant, which many people consider to be a weed. Not only are Monarchs losing their food but they're also losing where they like to live. They're also threatened by storms, droughts and other climate changes.

There is another type of Monarch Butterfly that lives only in South America. It isn't endangered. Some Monarch Butterfly species also live in Australia, Hawaii, Indonesia, on the Mediterranean coast and in the Canary Islands.

Moths

Like Butterflies, most Moth species are the only insects that have scales covering their wings. Another way Moths are different than other insects is they can curl up their feeding tube.

The easy way to tell the difference between Moths and Butterflies is by looking closely at their antennae. Moths have feathery antennae or they might look like threads. Butterflies have antennae with a round club tip.

Fun Bug Facts for Kids

This is a White Ermine Moth. It lives in the warmer parts of Europe and Asia.

Moths are known for having mostly dull colors, compared to the spectacular colors and patterns of Butterfly wings. But there are some moths that can compete as insect beauty queens with bright colors and patterns of their own.

Butterflies are daytime travellers, but most Moths are only out at night. It's the few daytime Moths that have the brightest colors. One of the most colorful types of Moths are the Tiger Moths with their brilliant reds and yellows.

Moths have an incredible sense of smell. Male moths can detect the scent of females over great distances.

Fun Bug Facts for Kids

This is a Death's Head Hawk Moth. It got its name from the markings on its upper back.

Many insects are strange eaters, but some Moths may be the strangest.

Lobocraspis griseifusa is a moth that lives deep in forests in Southeast Asia. To find it, first you would need to find a water buffalo. There will be a crowd of Moths near the water buffalo's eyes because this Moth lives by drinking its tears. It's not the only Moth species that lives on tears. The Moths that do this are picky eaters. They only choose slower-moving animals like those with hooves, such as cows, deer, and pigs. There are also Moths that sip Elephant tears.

Only half of the known species of Butterflies and Moths can hear. Among the ones who can hear, some are able to hear very high frequencies, above 300 kilohertz. That's the highest of any animal. Humans only hear sounds up to 20 kilohertz.

Moths with good hearing had it before bats developed their ultrasound hearing, but once the bats gained this advantage the Moths evolved so they could hear higher frequencies of sounds.

Tiger Moths defend themselves against the bats that attack them by using ultrasonic clicks that jam the bats' sonar.

All Moths are drawn to lights. Scientists haven't proven why but think it's because a bright light at night confuses the Moths.

The Giant Asian Hornet can fly 25 miles per hour, or 38.6 kilometres per hour.

This is a Hummingbird Hawk Moth.

Gypsy Moths

Gypsy Moths are a foreign invader. It happened because, back in the 1860s, there was a search for a hardy species of Moth to spin silk. But some of the lab Moths escaped (an insect talent), and 10 years later all the nearby trees were stripped of their leaves by this new Moth pest.

Since then, Gypsy Moths have done the same to millions of acres or hectares of trees and forests in Eastern United States and they are spreading. There is

Fun Bug Facts for Kids

Green Lacewings are on the good bugs list because they hunt and eat Mites and Aphids. Lacewings also eat plant nectar, pollen and are pollinators.

also a smaller group of Gypsy Moths on the Pacific coast.

They are so successful in spreading because their young larvae have hairs with air pockets. This allows them to float on the breeze, going great distances on windy days.

Gypsy Moths are also hitchhikers.

The female lays her eggs on recreation vehicles or trucks that are parked near trees. This is probably how Gypsy Moths first travelled from Massachusetts and that failed silk experiment to far-off Oregon and California.

Bug pests

Here are some of the reasons people get annoyed with bugs:

- Some bugs bite or sting. Their stings can be painful or itchy. For people who are allergic, these bugs can be deadly.
- Others attack and can destroy food crops, like Thrips and Wheat Weevils.
- Some, like Mosquitos, carry serious diseases.
- Others, like Termites, attack our buildings and homes, eating the wood and causing damage that costs a lot to fix.

A headless Cockroach only dies because it starves to death.

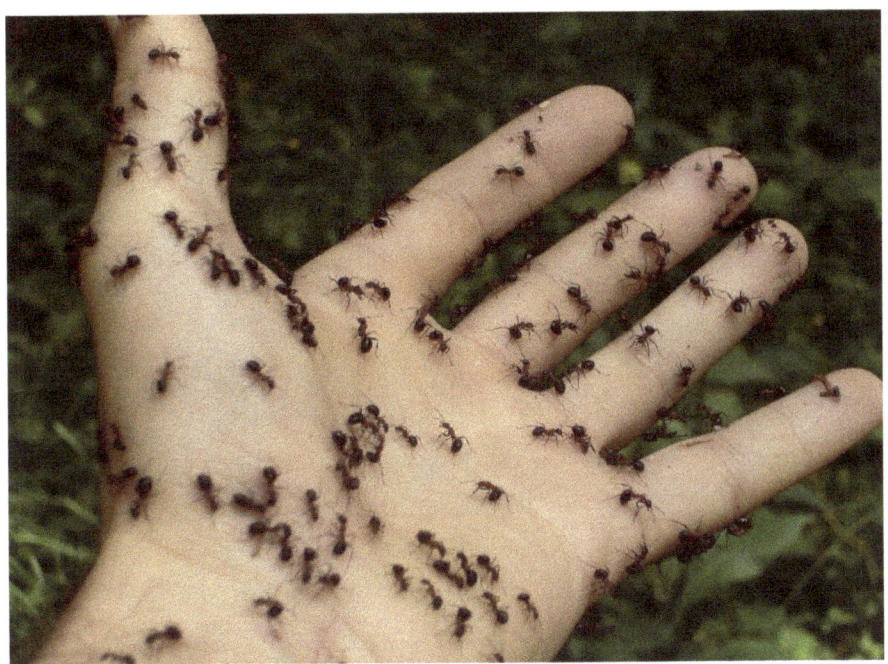

These are Wood Ants or Carpenter Ants. They're often mistaken for Termites. You can tell the difference because Carpenter Ants have pointed wings. Termite wings are much larger, twice as long as their bodies and they are shaped like paddles.

Ants

The first Ant was a Wasp that lost its wings. Among modern Ants, none of the workers can fly. Only the queen and her male suitors can fly. The males fly only during their very brief mating flights. The queen flies to find a new nesting site. Once she does, she bites off her own wings.

Ants have the largest brains in the insect world, compared to body size.

If you put every Ant in the world on one side of a balancing scale, and every human on the other side, the Ants would weigh more.

Ants are incredibly strong. All of them can carry things that weigh many times as much as they do. Asian Weaver Ants make their nests in trees. They've been seen carrying nest-building materials that weigh 100 times as much as they do. And they can do it while walking upside down!

All Ants are social. Every member of their community has a specific job to do. Some workers go out and search for food. Others wash and feed the larvae. They build vast underground tunnel cities. Thousands, and sometimes millions, of female workers live in their ant cities.

Ants can sense that an earthquake is coming as much as 24 hours before it happens. They do it by noticing changes in the earth's magnetic field.

Ants sleep at night, a lot like we do. Some of them sleep for 7 hours a night.

Exploding Ants

Exploding Ant workers make themselves explode when their home is attacked. They do it by splitting open their skin and spreading yellow goo on the attackers to confuse them and, sometimes, kill them.

Fun Bug Facts for Kids

An Ant can lift and carry more than 50 times its own weight. Common Garden Ants, like these Ants on a peony bud, live nearly everywhere in the world.

Driver Ants

The Driver Ants of Southern Africa are blind, but they have no trouble finding their prey. That's birds and small mammals. They have strong and enormous jaws that can still grip things after the Ants lose their heads. For this reason, Driver Ant heads are used by surgeons as staples to close wounds!

Fire Ants

Fire ants get their name from their burning sting, which can cause death for people who are allergic. They live in Southeastern United States and on the West Coast.

Bullet Ants

Bullet Ants are native to Central American and South America. They're a large black Ant that also delivers a painful sting that can kill humans.

Red Ants

The Red Ants that live in Kenya's forests are totally blind. That doesn't stop them from eating any creature in their path, including scorpions. They will even attack and eat elephants!

Some Ants have slaves

The only thing Amazon Ants know how to do is fight. Instead of learning how to feed themselves, Amazon Ants invade the colonies of other ants, kill their queen, then steal their larvae and pupae. When these kidnapped Ants become adults, they work for their Amazon Ant masters. But sometimes, these slave Ants revolt, rising up and killing their captors.

Amazon Ants don't live in the Amazon River basin. Instead, they live in Asia and some places in southern Europe.

Other Ant species send out hunters for Aphids. When a hunter Ant find Aphids, it leaves a scent trail to show worker Ants where to find the Aphids. The reason the Ants want them is Aphids excrete a sugary substance called honeydew. Ants eat the honeydew for energy. This is why they keep Aphid slaves.

Fun Bug Facts for Kids

A Termite mound in Africa.

The Ants use a tranquilizer drug on the Aphids. The Ants secret this drug from their feet. The drugged Aphids can't move as fast.

To get the honeydew, Ants use their Antennae to stroke the Aphids' abdomens, something like the way humans milk cows. When the Ants get really hungry, they eat the Aphids.

Termites

Termites look like Ants. Sometimes they're even called Termite Ants, but they aren't Ants. Termites are a type of Cockroach.

Most Termites are workers. Some worker Termites are blind, spending their entire lives underground.

A single Termite nest can have as many as 3 million Termites.

A Termite queen can lay many thousands of eggs in a day. The East African Termite queen lays 43,000 eggs in one day of laying. That's another egg every 2 seconds!

Queens live a long time, usually about 15 years although they can live up to 50 years.

While most of the 2,100 species of Termites stay small, there is an African Termite that can grow up to 5 inches or almost 13 centimetres long.

Termites damage buildings by eating the wood in the floors, walls and roof joists. They can be hard to spot before the damage is done because they're inside the walls.

Grasshoppers

These strong hoppers can do something most adult insects, and most animals, can't do. They can chew their food.

They hear through an organ on their abdomen and see with their 2 compound eyes but all their 3 simple eyes can do is tell the difference between light and dark. They have to molt five times as they grow from just born to adults.

Grasshoppers mostly live on the ground, jumping to get around. A full-grown adult Grasshopper or a

Most Grasshoppers in North America are the common green variety, but some in other parts of the world have more exotic colors, like these South African Red Grasshoppers.

Locust can jump a meter, or 39 inches, without using its wings. That's 20 times its own body length!

Many birds, small mammals, Bees, and Wasps eat Grasshoppers. They're also food for people in some parts of Asia. The science of studying Grasshoppers is called acridology.

All modern Bees, Ants and Wasps and Hornets evolved from one ancient ancestor insect. That ancestor was a Wasp. Over millions of years, some lost their wings and became vegetarians living in complex city-colonies. Today we call them Ants. Another group evolved to keep flying, also live in colonies and make honey – the Bees. And the third group are still very much like their ancient Wasp ancestor.

A swarm of Locusts can destroy a field of food crops in less than a day. They leave the fields stripped and bare, eating every part of the plant including the flowers, stems, leaves, fruit and seeds. They even eat bark.

Locusts

Locusts are actually grasshoppers gone rogue! When there are the right conditions for there to be a LOT of grasshoppers, the nymph behavior changes and they get bigger, becoming Locusts. Then they swarm.

In 1875, a swarm of Rocky Mountain Locusts 1,800 miles long and 110 miles wide, swarmed through the Western U.S. eating everything in their path and causing massive crop damage. This swarm had 3.5 trillion insects. It was the largest concentration of animals ever seen. But only 27 years later, Rocky Mountain Locusts were extinct.

Fun Bug Facts for Kids

Walking Sticks grow to be the longest insect alive today as adults. They can be 33 centimetres, or a foot long!

Damselflies are sometimes confused with Dragonflies. You can tell the difference because Dragonflies have wider, heavier bodies, while Damselflies, like these, are more delicate.

Damselflies

Like Dragonflies, Damselflies can bite and sting, but can't harm humans. Both can eat thousands of Mosquitoes a day. Along with bats, they are the world's best Mosquito controllers!

Dragonflies can live almost anywhere that's warm, but Damselflies only live near water. For most types of Damselflies, the male is more colorful than the female.

Kissing Bug

This South American bug has a pretty name but a deadly habit. They bite at night, usually close to a person's mouth, and their bite is deadly. This is because the bugs have parasites that carry a disease that has no cure. People who are bitten will have a damaged heart and could have a heart attack. The only known treatment is to get a heart transplant.

Assassin Bug

This bug got its scary name because the sting from its needle beak injects a victim insect with saliva. This saliva is a venom. It causes the victim's insides to turn to liquid which the Assassin Bug eats.

Can insects be pets?

Some insects can be temporary pets, like the Lightning Bugs you catch in a jar to see them up close. Then you let them go.

Or the cocoons you collect to see the Butterflies emerge, and then you watch them fly away.

There are a few insects that can make interesting pets that you could keep for longer. One is Ant farms, allowing you to see the Ants at work underground.

Another insect pet is Walking Sticks. They are the insect that has the largest eggs of any insect, more than 8 millimeters or a third of an inch long.

The only bug that lives in Antarctica is the Antarctic Midge. The adults can't fly and are barely larger than a flea. Even though it's tiny, it's the largest land animal alive today in Antarctica.

Fun Bug Facts for Kids

Fried Silkworks are a street food snack in Korea.

Insects for lunch!

Insects are full of proteins, minerals, and healthy fats. They're fairly easy to capture. In some parts of the world where chemical herbicides and pesticides aren't used there are lots of them, so they're cheap to buy, or you can catch your own. That's why, for 1 of every 3 people alive today, insects are a food they rely upon.

Most of these insect eaters live in the world's poorer or less developed countries.

In many places in Asia, insects are a street food snack.

School children don't just do their homework after school, they also collect bugs for the next day's school lunch. Children take the bugs they've caught to school, where all the bugs go into the frying pans for the school lunch shared by everyone.

Bugs can be used to make flour, like they do in southern Mexico with Grasshoppers used to make tortillas. In some countries, like Uganda, fried Grasshoppers are considered a special treat. They only appear twice a year, after the two rainy seasons. In other places, Termites and Cicadas are on the menu.

Some armed forces tell their members to eat bugs as a survival food.

Insects as food isn't a new thing. In the Bible, John the Baptist had a dinner of Locusts with honey, so we know that people have been eating insects for at least 2,000 years and probably much longer.

You might already be eating bugs without even knowing it. There are Grasshopper farms growing the insects to be added to food and protein supplements. Bugs are also in some pet foods.

Bugs are food for people in 80% of the world's nations.

Fun Bug Facts for Kids

When a chimpanzee gets a cut or wound, another will catch a Fly, squish it and put it on the wound. Somehow, chimps have learned that the bugs have antibacterial and anti-inflammatory benefits.

How do bugs help humans?

Here are some of the many ways humans benefit thanks to the bugs and insects:

- Bugs pollinate flowering plants.
- Some can help protect human food crops.
- Insects do most of the work to keep soil healthy.
- Some bugs are nutritious food for people and animals.
- Bugs have inspired inventions, such as human flight and paper.
- They produce honey, wax and silk.
- Bugs are nature's clean-up crew, getting rid of dead animals.
- Bugs can help to heal wounds.
- Many of them are beautiful and all of them are interesting.
- Bugs contribute to the biodiversity of our world.

You could help the bugs by building them a bug hotel like this one.

Bugs have always helped humans

We have been eating and enjoying honey and using beeswax for thousands of years.

There is also nothing new about Wasp venom as a medicine for people. It was used in ancient Greece, by the ancient Chinese and in Egypt thousands of years ago. But now researchers are learning new ways that insects can help with human health problems. One is in controlling inflammation, the root cause of many serious illnesses including rheumatoid arthritis.

Bee venom is used in treatments for sclerosis and tendonitis. Maggots are used in hospitals in Britain,

Plant milkweed in your yard or garden to feed Monarch Butterfly larvae.

Germany, Australia, China, Turkey and countries in Africa to clean wounds. It was common to use Maggots in wounds in American and Canadian hospitals during the last century, up until the 1930s when this practice stopped with the invention of antibiotics. Ancient civilizations also knew that wounds heal better when Maggots are used, including the Maya in Central America and Aboriginal Australians.

Here's how it works. The Maggots (or bug larvae) are put in a mesh wrapping, something like a tea bag. This bug bag is placed on a new wound for 4 days. The larvae eat the dead tissue in the wound, but don't eat healthy tissue. They also eat bacteria in the wound. The Maggots cannot bite. What they can do is clean a wound to make it heal faster.

Fun Bug Facts for Kids

Instead of a lawn, create a wildflower garden to feed the bugs and the birds!

Insects also help us with biocontrol.

This means using one 'good' creature to control another, destructive creature. Farmers have found it is cheaper and better to use Lady Bugs to eat crop-destroying Aphids, than to use pesticides on their fields.

Sniffer Wasps are more effective than dogs at sniffing out drugs, dead bodies and explosives. The Wasps are easier to train than dogs, they're more accurate, and they don't get tired as quickly as sniffer dogs do.

Some Mayfly eggs don't hatch for three years. Then they live their entire lives in just 6 hours!

Other bugs with benefits

Insect butter, insect cooking oil, insect cosmetics – it may sound incredible, but these are all real. So is Lac, a bug product made in India as an ingredient in printing inks, varnishes and sealants.

Beeswax is used to make candles, a base for ointments and in polishes for furniture. Beeswax is also used to make lipstick and other cosmetics.

The next time you eat cake, thank the bugs. They are in the coloring for cakes and icing. Natural insect dyes are also used to make clothing and in tanning for leather products.

Museum workers use Carpet Beetles to clean mammal skeletons for museum displays.

Mealworms are bug larvae that are food for reptile pets like bearded dragons and also farm animals including chickens and pigs.

Architects and engineers have learned how to build stronger structures by observing the hives of Honeybees. They also learned how to make our homes and buildings comfortably air-cooled by studying the hives of Termites. It is Butterflies who inspired the development of solar energy.

Polymer, made from dead Flies, can be turned into biodegradable plastic. The hard exoskeletons of insects, like the shells of shrimp and crabs, is made of chitlin, a sugar-based polymer. Bioplastics could help

This is a Jezebel Butterfly. Their home is in Asia.

us control, and possibly eventually eliminate the world's serious plastic pollution.

Are bugs endangered?

We need insects in our world to feed people and animals, to provide honey and wax, to inspire innovation, to help us learn better ways to treat injuries or illnesses, to be the cleanup crew for dead plants and animals and to keep the soil healthy.

Many of our insects are doing just fine, but some are endangered. Africanized Bees are killing native Bees. It could be that there will be no more Monarch

Butterflies in North America in your lifetime, despite our efforts to save them. Mexico has made their wintering homes a protected place, yet illegal logging continues. Long before they arrive at their winter home, the Butterflies are threatened in Canada and United States.

One way you can help the Monarchs is by planting milkweed in your yard or garden to feed their hungry larvae. Another would be to join the campaign to establish protected corridors through Canada and United States to Mexico, where no harsh chemical herbicides or pesticides would be allowed.

We have the need, the desire and the tools to save the Monarch Butterflies, if we can work together to save them.

But Monarchs aren't the only bugs who need our help! At least 66 insect species have become extinct since 1500. This is just the ones we know about, so there are probably more. Artificial lighting and light pollution, changes to the environment, shrinking habitats (that's where they live), expanding cities and increasing human populations (that means more people on earth) are also to blame. So are farming methods using pesticides and herbicides (bug-killers and weed-killers) and dangerous invader species like the Killer Bees.

We lose about 9% of our worldwide bug population every 10 years.

This means if we keep losing insects as fast as we are right now, by 2074 there will be half as many insects in the world as there are today. That would be a disaster for the world's people and animals. Losing our insects would cause worldwide famine. Many people, including in North America, wouldn't survive.

In some countries, researchers are developing bug replacements, like robot bees and drones that pollinate orchards. But is this really the answer? Or should we come together, as a world community, to save all the wonderful bugs we already have? We really do have a choice! And we already know that we can't survive without them.

How we can help the bugs

- Plant bug friendly gardens. Include some milkweed.
- Reduce light pollution. Lights confuse bugs and make them weaker.
- Change your lawn to be a wildflower meadow. Or plant wildflower gardens.
- If you must have grass, let it get longer. Cut it less often. Don't cut it at all in May to allow dandelions to bloom because they are the first food for the Bees in springtime in the Northern Hemisphere.
- Establish Monarch Butterfly migration corridors on the East Coast, from eastern Canada to Mexico.
- Leave piles of sticks to make a bug hotel.
- Put apple or orange slices on a plate or clean plant saucer to feed Butterflies.
- Ban pesticides and herbicides that harm insects and other animals.
- Use natural methods to control plant pests.

This is a Copper Butterfly.

Thank you!

Thanks for reading, and I hope you've enjoyed all these strange and amazing facts about bugs and insects.

If you want to know more about the most fascinating and fantastic creatures who share our world, turn the page!

Best wishes,

Jacquelyn

About Jacquelyn

Jacquelyn Elnor Johnson started telling stories to entertain her younger sisters, discovering in the telling what it takes to hold an audience! By age 15, she was a correspondent for the local newspaper and had written her first book. She went on to have careers in writing for and editing newspapers and magazines and teaching journalism.

A life-long pet lover, she is the bestselling author of 20 books about caring for and enjoying pets and animals, including **I Want A Bearded Dragon** and **Fun Snake Facts For Kids.**

Find more fun books at:
www.CrimsonHillBooks.com

Photo Credits

Thank you to:

Pixabay: Nicole Kohler, PollyDot, Jondolar Schnarr, Larisa Koshkina, Ronnie Overhate, Sunudda Lovanichaphat, Swamnil Angham, Ian Lindsay, Andreas Hoja, Danielle Eibrink Jansen, Josch13, Michael Reichelt, Liggraphy, Myriams-Fotos, Simon Oberthaler, David Hablutzel, Erik Karits, Claudia Wollesen, Antonios Ntoumas, Annette Meyer, Manolo Granco, PublicDomain Pictures, Dirk, Hans Braxmeier, AlexasFotos, Nimrod Orin, Warren Matthews, Ron Van den Berg, Lubos Houska, Rajesh Balouria, Robert Balog, Parlansky, Herbert Bieser, Ria, Jaggrz, Kjgalaxy, Marcel Langthim, Stawarzallegro, Eveline de Bruin, PopcornSusanN, Ilo and 12019.

Discover MORE about your favorite pets and animals in these books:

- **Fun Leopard Gecko and Bearded Dragon Facts for Kids**
- **Fun Reptile Facts for Kids**
- **Fun Dog Facts for Kids**
- **Fun Cat Facts for Kids**
- **Fun Pony Facts for Kids**
- **Fun Horse Facts for Kids**
- **Fun Bird Facts for Kids**
- **Fun Backyard Bird Facts for Kids**
- **Fun Dinosaur Facts for Kids**
- **Fun T-Rex Facts for Kids**
- **Fun Snake Facts for Kids**
- **Fun Bug Facts for Kids**
- **Fun Spider Facts for Kids**

www.ingramcontent.com/pod-product-compliance
Lightning Source LLC
Chambersburg PA
CBHW050730010526
44107CB00009B/800